APR 2 4 2014

EARTH'S TREASURES

SILVER

CHRISTINE PETERSEN
ABDO Publishing Company

visit us at
www.abdopublishing.com

Published by ABDO Publishing Company, PO Box 398166, Minneapolis, MN 55439.
Copyright © 2014 by Abdo Consulting Group, Inc. International copyrights reserved in all countries. No part of this book may be reproduced in any form without written permission from the publisher. The Checkerboard Library™ is a trademark and logo of ABDO Publishing Company.

Printed in the United States of America, North Mankato, Minnesota.
052013
092013

♻ PRINTED ON RECYCLED PAPER

Cover Photo: iStockphoto
Interior Photos: Alamy p. 19; AP Images pp. 21, 29; Corbis pp. 11, 13; Getty Images p. 15; iStockphoto pp. 1, 4, 8, 9, 12–13, 18, 25, 26–27; Science Source pp. 6, 7, 17, 22–23; Thinkstock pp. 5, 10

Editors: Rochelle Baltzer, Tamara L. Britton
Art Direction: Neil Klinepier

Library of Congress Control Number: 2013932672

Cataloging-in-Publication Data

Petersen, Christine.
 Silver / Christine Petersen.
  p. cm. -- (Earth's treasures)
ISBN 978-1-61783-874-3
Includes bibliographical references and index.
1. Silver--Juvenile literature. 2. Precious metals--Juvenile literature. I. Title.
669/.22--dc23

                                        2013932672

CONTENTS

TREASURE IN BATH

Have you ever visited a construction site? Bulldozers dig up the soil. Trucks roll in to pour a cement foundation. Cranes lift in huge steel beams. Before you know it, a new building has risen.

Construction is fascinating. But it also disturbs the landscape. This is why **archaeologists** were asked to visit a hotel construction site in Somerset, England. The city of Bath is built on the ruins of a 2,000-year-old Roman spa. Historical objects often turn up in the soil. So, archaeologists were glad for the opportunity to investigate the area before the hotel was built.

Work began in 2007. Just below ground level the archaeologists found the remains of a Roman building. A box had been hidden in its floor. Inside were more than 22,000 silver coins.

Many hoards of Roman coins have been found in Britain. The Beau Street Hoard is one of the five largest.

The coins became known as the Beau Street **Hoard**.

The most recent coins had been **minted** in the year 274 CE. But one was from 32 BCE! The hoard was an important historical find. But why was all this money left behind? No one will ever know.

The spa at Bath was called Aquae Sulis.

5

What Is Silver?

For at least 5,000 years, humans have used silver and other metals to make beautiful and useful things. Metals are chemical elements that occur naturally. We collect them from the earth by mining.

Each chemical element contains one kind of atom. Atoms are so small they cannot be seen except with the most powerful microscopes. Yet they form everything in our universe. This is possible because atoms bond together. They are kind of like building blocks in a toy construction kit!

In minerals, atoms bond in a repeating pattern. This pattern produces a three-dimensional shape called a crystal. A crystal can grow as more atoms join the pattern.

Most minerals are built from at least two elements. There are more than 100 elements. Imagine

A silver atom's nucleus consists of 47 protons (red) and 60 neutrons (blue). The 47 electrons (green) bind to the nucleus.

the many combinations they can make! For example, the mineral galena is made from atoms of lead and sulfur. Chalcopyrite has copper, iron, and sulfur atoms. A few minerals contain only one kind of atom. These are called native minerals. Silver is one of these.

All crystals of the same mineral have the same basic shape. Galena crystals tend to have eight sides. Some grow as long as your hand. By contrast, you would need a magnifying glass to see individual crystals of silver. Silver crystals usually clump together. They look like grains, plates, or long wires.

MAKING MONEY

Silver has many qualities that make the metal useful. It is solid at room temperature. Yet, it is soft enough that simple tools will mark and cut it. Warmed silver can be twisted and bent into many shapes. When heated to 1,764 degrees Fahrenheit (962°C) it will melt.

Ancient **smiths** used this knowledge to **mint** silver coins. The smith started with a two-piece mold. Each piece of the mold showed one side of the coin. He melted a small piece of silver and poured it into the bottom of the mold. The other half of the mold was quickly placed on top.

While the metal was still hot, the smith hit the

Silver often flowed unevenly in the mold. So, many coins were uneven and cracked around the edge.

Silver for investment is 99.9 percent pure. It is stamped 999.

8

mold with a hammer. Silver flowed through the mold. The new coin was allowed to cool and harden. Many identical coins could be produced this way.

Silver was the ideal metal for these early coins. Gold was used to make the emperor's own money. Copper coins were less expensive to make. But, copper becomes green and scaly as it reacts with air and water. This **corrosion** eventually destroys copper objects.

Today, half dollars, quarters, and dimes in the United States are 91.67 percent copper and 8.33 percent nickel.

Until 1964, they were 90 percent silver and 10 percent copper.

9

WORKS OF ART

Silversmiths were important craftspeople in Colonial America. They made objects such as silverware, teapots, and cups. For most citizens, these items were made of less expensive metals. But in more prosperous homes, silver objects were a popular sign of wealth.

To create a silver object, the smith hammered silver **ingots** into thin sheets. He placed these sheets over **stakes** and further pounded them to create rounded shapes. The smith used sharp objects to punch holes in the metal. Some objects were **engraved** with decorative patterns.

Silver does not absorb light, it reflects it. This makes silver appear to be white.

10

Handles were molded and **soldered** to objects such as teapots. The ends of the finished handles were heated in a flame. The spot where it would be attached was also heated. The two pieces were held together until they cooled.

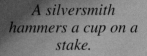

A silversmith hammers a cup on a stake.

Today, Native Americans are among the world's finest **silversmiths**. Many of their jewelry designs begin with simple sheets of **sterling silver**. Sterling silver is stronger than pure silver and less expensive.

Tarnish is a red to black colored coating that develops on the surface of silver. It is caused by exposure to sulfides in the air.

12

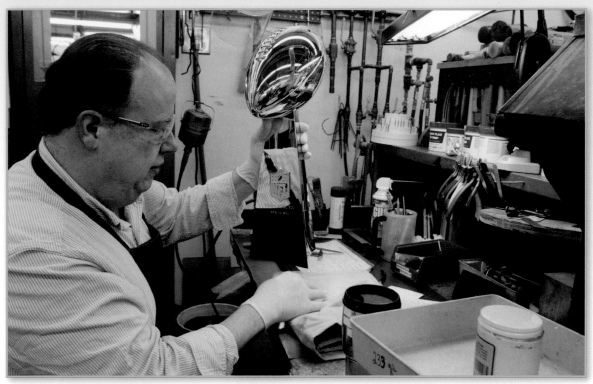

Each year, silversmiths at Tiffany & Company craft the Vince Lombardi Trophy from sterling silver. The trophy is awarded to the winner of the NFL's championship game, the Super Bowl.

The **silversmith** draws a pattern on a silver sheet. The pattern is cut using a threadlike saw. The design may be **soldered** onto another piece of metal. Or, it may be made into smaller pieces of jewelry. The final product is polished until it shines like moonlight.

Mirror, Mirror

Polished silver is more reflective than any other natural substance. Very little light is absorbed by its surface. Instead, light bounces away. This **luster** makes silver objects seem to glow with white light.

Ancient Egyptians took advantage of this quality. They melted silver and copper to form an **alloy**. It was hammered into flat, sturdy plates. These may have been the first mirrors. Some had decorative handles, making the mirror easy to hold and look into.

Today, silver remains an **essential** ingredient in the manufacture of mirrors. Mirrors are made from sheets of glass. But, silver will not stick to glass. So, an alloy of tin and silver must be used.

The glass is gently heated. One side is sprayed with a thin coat of liquid that contains tin. Then, silver is applied evenly over the tin layer.

Plain glass is transparent. You can see right through it. A mirror is different. Light reflects off its smooth layer of silver. In it, you can see your own reflection.

Almost all the light that hits silver is reflected back. This is called reflectivity. Mirrors work because silver has a reflectivity of 95 to 100 percent.

SHINE ON

The Gemini South **observatory** is located in the South American country of Chile. Gemini North is located in Hawaii. Together, they can observe almost all of the sky.

Like all machines, telescopes generate heat as they work. This heat results in **noise**. Noise affects a telescope's ability to make clear pictures.

Unlike commercial mirrors, most astronomical mirrors are coated with aluminum. However, in addition to reflecting light, silver also reflects heat. So in 2004, **astronomers** at Gemini South decided to coat their telescope mirrors with silver.

The project began with the largest of three mirrors. It is 26.6 feet (8.1 m) in **diameter**. The glass was coated with four layers of silver. Each layer was 200 times thinner than a human hair! It took only 2 ounces (50 grams) of silver to complete the job.

Today, all of Gemini South's telescope mirrors are coated with silver. The telescopes produce less heat and noise. So, they can take clearer images of deep space!

Gemini South scientists photographed the stars forming in the center of this nebula.

HIT THE SWITCH

All metals are good **conductors**. Heat and electricity pass through them easily. Silver is the best conductor of all. Manufacturers take advantage of this quality in many ways.

How many electronic devices are in your home? Most of these run on batteries. The small, round "button" batteries in toys, watches, and cameras often contain silver oxide.

Laptops and cell phones typically use lithium ion batteries. These batteries produce a lot of power. But they can explode if the device gets too hot.

In addition to silver, computers contain gold, platinum, and copper.

New batteries made from a silver-zinc **alloy** may be a good replacement. They cannot catch on fire.

Silver is in dozens of other electronics that you use every day. Did you flip a light switch this morning? Silver helped carry electricity through that switch. Silver is also used to make parts in television remote controls, computer keyboards, and microwave ovens. And, every electrical action in a modern car is activated with silver-coated **contacts**.

The water pipes in your home may be coated with a silver-tin alloy. The coating makes pipes stronger. It controls temperature when they carry hot water. Silver does not **corrode**. So, using silver means that all these products last longer.

HEALING POWER

Silver is useful in much more than manufacturing. It can also keep us healthy. More than 3,000 years ago, the people of Phoenicia made jars from silver. They stored water and milk in the jars. The liquids rarely spoiled.

The ancient Phoenicians did not understand why the silver jars prevented spoilage. They just noticed the benefit and took advantage of it.

Today, modern scientists understand that silver absorbs oxygen molecules. Many types of bacteria and mold need oxygen to survive. Without oxygen, these organisms die. Water purification systems using silver can kill dangerous bacteria and keep people healthy.

Cream containing silver restricts bacterial growth in severe burns. But, silver does not only kill bacteria. It also helps the body heal faster. Have you recently covered a wound with an adhesive bandage? That bandage may have contained a small amount of silver!

Some hospitals use cleaning products that contain silver. These kill many kinds of bacteria. Silver can even be built into medical instruments and furniture used in hospitals.

Fabric made with silver kills bacteria. This helps control odor.

SILVER'S SOURCE

Silver is a useful resource. However, it is scarce. Scientists have calculated that silver occurs at an average rate of five parts per million. Imagine collecting a sample of rock. For every million atoms in that rock, only five would be of silver.

So, how do large silver deposits form? Below Earth's surface is a layer called the mantle. The mantle contains hot, liquid rock called magma. Sometimes, magma erupts upward. It may emerge as a volcano. Or, it may stop within the rocky crust just below Earth's surface.

As the magma cools underground, it releases salty water. The water flows through cracks and spaces in the crust. It eats

EARTH'S LAYERS

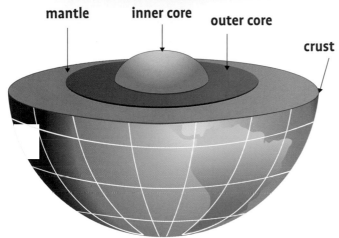

mantle   inner core   outer core   crust

away at the rock. Atoms of metals and other elements are released and carried along in the fluid.

The water may become trapped in narrow cracks between rock layers. It can also seep through holes in the seafloor. In either case, minerals form as they separate from the water.

Silver tends to mix with sulfur, lead, copper, and zinc. These mineral deposits are known as ores. Ores contain valuable amounts of metals that can be mined.

The International Union of Pure and Applied Chemistry recognizes 114 elements. Silver is the sixty-eighth most abundant element in Earth's crust.

23

MINING SILVER

In 1859, gold miners were working on a small mountain range in western Nevada. They dug into a layer of sticky blue mud. It was full of silver! The miners called it the Comstock Lode. It was the first important silver deposit mined in the United States.

The miners collected the mud with their shovels. When that was gone, they dug shafts deep into the earth to find more silver. These mines were dangerous. But nothing stopped the miners from digging until the ore ran out.

Modern silver mining uses heavy equipment and technology. In surface mines, the ground is blasted with explosives so the ore can be removed. The rock is cut away in layers, each deeper than the last. Silver ores can also be removed from deposits far below the surface.

About 55 different ores contain some amount of silver. For example, silver is mixed with sulfur in acanthite and lead in galena. After an ore is mined, the metals must be separated. This step requires chemicals, heat, or electricity.

Today in the United States, silver is mined in Alaska, Nevada, and Idaho. The world's most productive silver mines are located in Mexico, Peru, and China. The largest is in Australia.

The rock layers of a surface mine are called benches. They look like the steps of a stadium. These mines are also called open-pit mines.

North
America

South
America

**Top Silver-
Producing Countries**

Australia   Mexico

Bolivia   Peru

Canada   Poland

Chile   Russia

China   United
States

MINER FOR A DAY

Though much safer, modern mines are still dangerous places. So, they are rarely open to visitors. But you can still experience the history of silver mining.

Sierra Silver Mine is located in the Coeur d'Alene mountains of Idaho. There, you can put on a hard hat and walk deep into the mountain. Silver has been mined there since the 1880s. You will learn how silver was mined in the past and see equipment used today. And you will receive a sample of ore to take home!

Become a Rock Hound!

WOULD YOU LIKE TO START YOUR OWN COLLECTION OF GEMS AND MINERALS? BECOME A ROCK HOUND!

To get started, locate a site likely to have the treasures you seek. Before you head out, be sure it is legal and you have permission to collect specimens from your search area. Then, gather the tools and safety gear you'll need. Don't forget to bring an adult!

Label your treasures with the date and location you found them. Many rock hounds set a goal for their collections. For example, they might gather samples of all the minerals found in their state or province.

Finally, always leave the land in better shape than you found it. Respecting the environment helps preserve it for future rock hounds and the rest of your community.

WHAT WILL YOU NEED?
map
compass
magnifying glass
hard hat or bicycle helmet
safety goggles
sunscreen
bucket
shovel
rock hammer
pan or screen box
containers for your finds

Water in the flume washes dirt and sand away leaving Earth's treasures behind.

Looking for a bigger challenge? Visit the Someplace Special Gem Mine in West Virginia. There, you can buy a bucket filled with dirt. You put the dirt in a screen box, then wash it in a flume. It's just like miners did in the old days!

Silver is called a precious metal for good reason. There is a limited supply on our planet. However, its use in products such as jewelry, electronics, and batteries is increasing. Wise use today will allow people to enjoy the benefits of silver long into the future.

GLOSSARY

alloy - a metal made by melting two or more metals, or a metal and another material, and mixing them together.

archaeologist (ahr-kee-AH-luh-jihst) - one who studies the remains of people and activities from ancient times.

astronomer (uh-STRAH-nuh-muhr) - one who studies objects and matter outside Earth's atmosphere.

conductor - a material that permits an electric current to flow easily.

contact - the meeting place of two points in an electrical system through which current passes.

corrode - to wear away gradually by chemical action.

diameter - the distance across the middle of an object, such as a circle.

engrave - to cut or carve figures, letters, or designs into a hard surface.

essential - very important or necessary.

hoard - a supply of something, often valuable, that is stored up and hidden away.

ingot (IHNG-guht) - a piece of metal made into a particular shape so that it is easy to handle or shape.

luster - a shiny quality, especially from reflected light.

mint - to make coins out of pieces of metal.

noise - inconsistent operation of a device due to interference by heat.

observatory - a place or a building for observing the weather or the stars.

smith - an artisan who makes things out of metal. Silversmiths work with silver.

solder (SAH-duhr) - a mixture of metals that is melted and used to join metal parts together. To solder is to unite or repair using solder.

stake - a polished iron or steel tool over which metal is shaped.

sterling silver - a mixture of 92.5 percent silver and 7.5 percent copper.

SAYING IT

acanthite - uh-KAHN-thite
chalcopyrite - kal-kuh-PEYE-rite
Coeur d'Alene - kawrd-uhl-AYN

WEB SITES

To learn more about silver, visit ABDO Publishing Company online. Web sites about silver are featured on our Book Links page. These links are routinely monitored and updated to provide the most current information available.

www.abdopublishing.com

INDEX